ITHACA THEN & NOW

(c.1867)

(1983)

East Hill and South Hill from atop Cascadilla Hall

ITHACA THEN & NOW

by Merrill Hesch and Richard Pieper

Historic Views from the Collection
of the DeWitt Historical Society of Tompkins County
Rephotographed Today

McBooks Press • Ithaca, New York 14850

Book design by Mary A. Scott
Cover photographs by Seth L. Sheldon and Richard Pieper
Back cover photograph by Seth L. Sheldon
Typesetting by Strehle's Computerized Typesetting
Printing by Salina Press

This publication is made possible in part by grants from the Bowers Foundation, the Eva Gebhard-Gourgaud Foundation, the Cecil Howard Charitable Trust, and the New York State Council on the Arts, a state agency, through the help of the Tompkins County Arts Council, Ithaca, New York.

Library of Congress Cataloging in Publication Data

Hesch, Merrill, 1955-
    Ithaca then & now.

    Bibliography: p.
    1. Ithaca (N.Y.)--Description--Views.   2. Ithaca
(N.Y.)--Buildings--Pictorial works.   3. Historic
buildings--New York (State)--Ithaca--Pictorial works.
4. Ithaca (N.Y.)--History--Pictorial works.   I. Pieper,
Richard, 1950-   . II. DeWitt Historical Society of
Tompkins County.   III. Title.   IV. Title: Ithaca then and
now.
F129.I8H47   1983   974.7'71   83-19912
ISBN 0-935526-10-2 (pbk.)

This book is available to the book trade from McBooks Press, 106 North Aurora Street, Ithaca, NY 14850. Individuals may order this book from bookstores or directly from McBooks Press. Please include $1.00 postage and handling with mail orders.

Printed in the United States of America
9 8 7 6 5 4 3 2 1

To Seth L. Sheldon, Ellsworth McGillvray,
Joseph C. Burritt, Robert G. Estabrook,
Henry Head, and the other photographers,
whose views of a changing city
made this project possible.

ACKNOWLEDGMENTS

We are greatly indebted to the friends and acquaintances without whose assistance this project could not have been completed. Special thanks go to the staff of the DeWitt Historical Society of Tompkins County for their patience and kindness during these many months of work. Director Craig Williams, who was never without helpful information, and Carl Koski, who printed glass plates and copied historic views, deserve special mention. Jon Crispin and Jon Reis, friends and photographers, provided advice, technical assistance, and the generous loan of darkroom space, which contributed immeasurably to the quality of the contemporary photographs. Tania Werbizky reviewed text and photographs, and provided valuable editorial advice during innumerable late night work sessions. In addition to the staff of the DeWitt Historical Society, research assistance was provided by Andrea Lazarski, Nick Langhart, Mary Raddant Tomlan, and Michael Tomlan. The Morse Chain Company, Citizens Savings Bank, David Morgan, Harry Simrell and Pete Zaharis provided access to roofs and high points for the contemporary photographs. Anne Solomon and Natalie de Combray typed much of the text. We would like to thank Carol Sisler, former Director of Historic Ithaca, and the staff of the Tompkins County Arts Council for their support and assistance in the initial phases of this project. Jill Chambers-Hartz and Zan Sawyer-Dailey provided aid with grant applications and budgetary planning. Finally we thank designer Mary A. Scott who made the sensitive transition from concept to book, editor Katharyn Machan Aal, and publisher Alex Skutt, who provided assistance and advice, and who shared our interest in things past.

The research and photography for this project would not have been possible without the generous financial contributions of the New York State Council on the Arts, the Bowers Foundation, the Eva Gebhard-Gourgaud Foundation, and the Cecil Howard Charitable Trust.

INTRODUCTION

ITHACA, like much of America, has in recent years experienced a growing awareness of its architectural heritage. Part of this appreciation has been the renaissance of architectural photography and a renewed interest in the work of late nineteenth century photographers. In Ithaca, historic photographs now hang in bank lobbies, restaurants, and bars. Many of these scenes are easily recognizable, although drastic changes in the built environment have occurred; new streets have been constructed, nineteenth century landmarks have been demolished to make way for modern structures, and other historic buildings have undergone major renovation. Often areas have changed so completely that early views can be identified only by assiduous historians or long-term residents.

Within the past ten years, many cities have been the subject of "Then and Now" books, pairing historic photographs with contemporary views taken from the same vantage point. These comparisons, accompanied by explanatory text, vividly display the vast architectural changes that urban areas have undergone. Such books can also serve to raise a community's historic preservation awareness. *Ithaca Then and Now* was conceived with this goal in mind.

Turn of the century Ithaca was a prosperous community undergoing rapid changes. Numerous photographers intentionally recorded the construction and catastrophe that changed Ithaca's cityscape, while others inadvertently captured moments in architectural history in their prints—a view of an Aurora Street parade reveals as much about the buildings of the time as it does about the event it was meant to record.

The photographic research that led to this selection of views was at once exhilarating and heartbreaking as an image of a city in flux unfolded. The historic photographs reproduced here, taken from the collection of the DeWitt Historical Society of Tompkins County, were selected with a number of criteria in mind, including historic significance, geographic distribution and photographic quality. Many favorite views were excluded because the contemporary view was uninteresting or could not be photographed from the same vantage point.

The book is weighted to downtown scenes, for that is where the most significant and striking changes have occurred, and seemingly where most photographs were taken. Views of residential neighborhoods, South Hill and Fall Creek, for example, are surprisingly scarce. The historic photographs selected date from about 1866 to 1934, though most were taken in the two decades at the turn of the twentieth century. Though their names are hardly well known, the work of Ithaca photographers Seth L. Sheldon, Ellsworth McGillvray, Joseph C. Burritt and Robert G. Estabrook is featured prominently in this publication. Inevitably, with a book of this size, there are omissions; apologies are extended to those who have a favorite view or neighborhood that is not included.

No printed reproduction can do justice to the wealth of detail found in the original photographs, many of which are contact prints from large glass plates. New prints from original negatives were used whenever possible but some extraordinary views have been reproduced from old photographic prints, with an understandable loss in image quality. To preserve the integrity of the historic images, minimal cropping was done, and tears, stains and vignetted corners are visible in some views.

To duplicate the perspective of the historic photographs, a view camera with 65 mm, 90 mm, and 135 mm lenses was used for contemporary photography. Both 2¼ × 2¾ in. and 4 × 5 in. formats were employed. Every effort was made to duplicate original camera placement and framing, but where trees, wires, traffic signals or even buildings have blocked the view, the camera was moved. In some cases differences in photographic equipment have resulted in differences in perspective, with near or distant buildings distorted in size. All current photographs were taken by Richard Pieper between March and August of 1983.

The considerable research that contributed to the dating and description of these views was conducted by Merrill Hesch. Ithaca directories, nineteenth and twentieth century maps, books on local history, newspaper clippings, and scrapbook and manuscript collections of the DeWitt Historical Society provided the background for the accompanying text. A bibliography has been included for those wishing more information on the growth and development of the City of Ithaca.

Fitting together the pieces of this historical puzzle has been a challenging and enjoyable experience. There is a special excitement to uncovering an article in a yellowed newspaper or standing in the footsteps of an earlier photographer. This volume is a distillation of thousands of photographs and scores of histories that together present an image of Ithaca's past. It is a testimony to the City's history, with an eye to the changes in its future.

Ithaca, 1983   Merrill Hesch and Richard Pieper

Aurora Street, Looking South from State Street (c.1870)

MUCH OF ITHACA'S early trade came overland from Owego, a major Susquehanna River port located thirty miles to the south. The passage of the Owego Turnpike along Hudson Street contributed greatly to the early settlement of South Hill. Prominent residences lined Prospect, Pleasant and Columbia Streets by the early 1850's. Ithaca's commercial establishments at that time clustered around the intersection of Aurora and State Streets and numerous shops and industries could be found at the base of the two hills. Businesses catering to travellers included the Lewis Brothers livery and the National Hotel. The large building at the base of the creek in this view was Stoddard's tannery. A few carriages abandoned in the snow across the street may have been awaiting repair at A. S. Cowdry's carriage shop. The large wooden building in the right foreground is the original Ithaca Hotel, erected in 1809 by Luther Gere.

Aurora Street, Looking South from State Street

ALTHOUGH ITHACA'S commercial core eventually moved further west to the intersection of State and Tioga Streets, South Aurora Street remained an important commercial center. The extension of Green Street to State Street in 1956 required the demolition of the structures to the north of the creek and a grade change to accommodate the new roadway beneath the Six Mile Creek bridge. The second Ithaca Hotel, a brick building which replaced the earlier wooden structure, was demolished in 1968. A new Rothschild's department store immediately to the right of this view, was constructed on the lot in 1975. The business office of the New York Telephone Company, located in the left foreground, was erected one year later.

Ithaca Hotel, Southwest Corner of State and Aurora Streets (1898-1904)

THE ITHACA HOTEL, at the southwest corner of State and Aurora Streets, was a landmark to generations of Ithacans. Designed by local architect Alfred B. Dale and erected in 1872 at a cost of $64,000, this brick block replaced an earlier three story wooden hotel of the same name that had been destroyed by the great State Street fire of 1871. This hotel provided accommodations for 200 guests and 175 diners and in 1891 was known for its "spacious parlors, reading, reception, billiard and sample rooms."[1] In 1898 the building was renovated and reopened as the New Ithaca Hotel under the supervision of proprietor Alva H. Gluck. Its popular grill room, the Dutch Kitchen, was installed at that time under the direction of Ithaca architect William Henry Miller. The three buildings to the left on Aurora Street were all saloons when this photograph was taken. The Chacona Candy Store occupied the columned storefront to the right.

Rothschild's Department Store, Southwest Corner of State and Aurora Streets

THE ITHACA HOTEL was purchased in 1958 by the Ithaca Hotel Corporation. For the next 10 years the owners wrestled with various development schemes for the site. Initially a new hotel was planned, and in March of 1968 demolition of the Ithaca Hotel began. Doors and panels from the Dutch Kitchen were salvaged and installed in the Ramada Inn on South Cayuga Street. The site remained empty for a number of years. In 1973 the city accepted a development proposal from the Caldwell Corporation calling for the erection of a new Rothschild's department store, a hotel, and a 400 car two-tier parking garage. Construction of the department store and garage was completed in 1975, though the hotel was never built. The Rothschild's building was designed by the New York firm Warner, Burns, Toan and Lunde.

Northeast Corner of State and Aurora Streets (c.1908)

DANIEL H. WANZER and Frederick G. Manley founded a grocery store in 1869 at 103 North Aurora Street, then a three story building. Five years later Wanzer became the business owner and by 1890 had opened an additional shop in the four-story brick building around the corner at 304 East State Street. Wanzer operated the business alone until 1899 when it was purchased by his son Elmer and Sydney Howell. In 1905 Elmer Wanzer erected on the corner lot a new structure designed by Arthur Gibb. He also joined the two neighboring buildings together creating one blockfront by extending the cornice from 304 East State Street across all three facades and adding a fourth floor to 103 North Aurora Street. The Lehigh Valley Railroad Company moved their ticket office into the ground floor. To the left of the block at 105-107 North Aurora Street stood an office building erected for the Postal Telegraph Cable Company in 1904. The small building immediately to the right of the Wanzer Block housed the Burns Brothers blacksmith shop.

Northeast Corner of State and Aurora Streets

D ANIEL H. WANZER died in 1921 at the age of 84. Elmer continued to operate the two grocery stores until 1930. The Lehigh Valley Railroad Company's ticket office remained in the Wanzer block until 1960. The Postal Telegraph building was sold and converted to a hotel in 1950, later known as the Hotel Leonardo. In 1916 the blacksmith shop at 306-308 E. State Street was demolished and replaced by the White Building, erected by L. S. White for use as a photographic studio. Andrews Confectionary Shop, opened in 1931 by Anthony Andrews, and still operated by his widow Ruby Andrews, continues to occupy its original storefront at 308 East State Street. Shown on the extreme right is the Strand Theatre, erected in 1917 at 310-312 East State Street, "unsur-passed by any theatre in the United States in completeness and attractiveness" as reported by the *Ithaca Journal* on opening night April 23, 1917. Driscoll Brothers of Ithaca designed and built this Jacobean Revival style theatre, capable of seating 1,650 people. The Strand is remembered as the city's most noted stage for drama including performances by Orson Welles, Katherine Cornell and Basil Rathbone in *The Barretts of Wimpole Street* (1934), Clare Booth in *The Women* (1937), and Katherine Hepburn and Van Heflin in *The Philadelphia Story* (1940). The Strand closed as a movie theatre in 1975. Partially restored for theatrical use, plans for the building's reopening are under consideration.

West Side of Aurora Street Looking North from State Street (c.1898)

THIS PHOTOGRAPH of an unidentified parade on North Aurora Street presents a glimpse of life in Ithaca circa 1898. Unlike the annual Ithaca Fire Department parades and inspections, this parade featured horse-drawn displays by local businesses, such as the paper display by Enz and Miller, the wholesale paper company founded in 1878 and the predecessors to T. G. Miller's Sons Paper Company. This block of North Aurora Street is anchored by two substantial brick buildings, both designed by Alfred B. Dale in the early 1870's. The Griffen Block, the large four story building in the left corner of this photograph, was built in 1878 for William H. Griffen, a city councilman and insurance agent, replacing an earlier building destroyed in the State Street fire of 1871. The Bates Block, located at the corner of East Seneca Street, was erected in 1872 for Rufus Bates, a grocer. The three story building at 108-110 North Aurora Street next to the Griffen Block contained the original Lager Beer Saloon and Restaurant operated by Theodore Zinck. The small two story boot and shoe store next door at 112 North Aurora Street was operated by Patrick and Frank Wall, who opened for business at this location around 1873.

West Side of Aurora Street Looking North from State Street

In 1974 the ground floor of the Griffen Block was restored and now houses a bar, Simeon's. Five years later, after a fire destroyed the upper two floors, the Bates Block was renovated and painted, highlighting its original cast iron details. Theodore Zinck, distraught over the death of his daughter in the typhoid epidemic of 1903, drowned himself in Cayuga Lake later that year. The restaurant, under new management, relocated several times, closing finally in 1967. Zinck's Saloon remains immortalized in the Cornell song sung to the tune of "Give My Regards To Broadway" and ending "We'll all have drinks/At Theodore Zinck's/When I get back next fall."

Tompkins House, Northwest Corner of Seneca and Aurora Streets (c.1910)

AT THE NORTHWEST corner of Seneca and Aurora Streets stood the Tompkins House, a popular hostelry in Ithaca for 125 years. About 1806 Jacob Vrooman built a public house, originally known as the Ithaca Hotel, on the site. In 1809, in honor of Governor Daniel Tompkins, he changed the name of the inn to Tompkins House. A new one-and-one-half-story inn was built on the same site and re-christened the Tompkins House in 1832. In 1865 the building was enlarged to four stories and renovated under the direction of Samuel Holmes and his son-in-law A. B. Stamp. The hotel contained 72 sleeping rooms and could seat 75 diners. Room rates were $1.50 per day in 1891. The livery for the hotel was replaced in 1907 by the building with a columned facade to the west on Seneca Street. Designed by Gibb and Waltz, the Neo-classical style structure housed John Reamer's Modern Method Laundry and Clarence Head's shirt factory.

Seneca Street Parking Ramp, Northwest Corner of Seneca and Aurora Streets

THE TOMPKINS HOUSE along with neighboring structures fell to the wrecker's ball in 1957 to make way for a municipal parking lot. The Seneca Street parking ramp, built in 1974, occupies the site today.

Intersection of Seneca and Tioga Streets Looking South (c.1900)

BY THE END of the nineteenth century the commercial core of Ithaca centered around the intersection of State and Tioga Streets. The 100 block of North Tioga Street contained many of Ithaca's prominent buildings and established institutions. On the left stood the Cornell Library, predecessor to the Tompkins County Public Library, erected by Ezra Cornell in 1863 and designed by William Hodgins of Albany. It was one of many civic projects that Cornell financed. Dedication of the building took place in the auditorium, known as Library Hall, on December 20, 1866. The first commencement exercises for Cornell University were held in the hall in 1869. Susan B. Anthony, Elizabeth Cady Stanton, and Mark Twain were among the distinguished visitors who lectured there. Adjacent to the library stood the Masonic Block, erected in 1870 and designed by Alfred B. Dale. On the corner at the right of this view stood the Ithaca Savings Bank. From 1878 until 1887 the Bank conducted business in a brick dwelling on this site owned by ex-Governor Alonzo B. Cornell, Ezra's son. In 1887 the bank erected this new building designed by William Henry Miller. The Ithaca Trust Company first opened an office in the Savings Bank Building in 1891. Soon thereafter Arthur Gibb was commissioned to design a new headquarters, and in 1895 the Trust Company moved next door to 110 North Tioga Street.

Intersection of Seneca and Tioga Streets Looking South

THIS BLOCK of downtown has undergone numerous changes. The Cornell Library was demolished in 1960. The Masonic Block was replaced by the First Bank of Ithaca in 1932. On May 4, 1921, the Ithaca Savings Bank was badly damaged by fire and was demolished. The present Citizens Savings Bank was designed by Gibb and Waltz and erected in 1924. The Ithaca Trust Company at 110 North Tioga Street became the Tompkins County Trust Company in 1935 following its merger with the Tompkins County National Bank.

East Side of Tioga Street Looking North from Seneca Street (c.1915)

FIRES IN JUNE of 1840 and July of 1842 destroyed a number of buildings on the north and south sides of Owego (now State) Street. At a meeting held in the Clinton House, village president John James Speed urged the erection of a village hall to house all fire equipment under one roof; his motion was approved unanimously. Soon after the Board of Trustees purchased the lot at the northeast corner of Seneca and Tioga Streets for $1800 from George McCormick. McCormick's residence was moved to the lot directly north in the center of this photograph. It was later used as the village hall annex. On February 4, 1844, the new hall was formally opened to the public. Throughout the nineteenth century the basement held the fire department and the upper floor provided space for public gatherings, concerts, and dramatic entertainment. Some of Ithaca's earliest theatrical productions were staged in the hall, including the "Celebrated Diorama of the Burning of Moscow, together with an amusing scene in ventriloquism by Mr. Gallagher"[2] in May of 1852 and the American Ballet Troupe in January of 1856. By the turn of the century the building housed the police and fire department headquarters, the Mayor's office, the City Clerk's office and City Hall. In July of 1896 the Women's Christian Temperance Union unveiled a public drinking fountain on the corner "equipped with faucets and bowls for the accommodation of man, horse and dog."[3] The bronzed iron fountain, surmounted by a statue of Hebe, cupbearer to the gods and goddesses of Mount Olympus, dispensed water cooled by a special receptacle of ice and provided the thirsty with an alternative to the nearby saloons.

East Side of Tioga Street Looking North from Seneca Street

PUBLIC DISCUSSION regarding the need for a new City Hall began as early as the 1890's. Some viewed the Greek Revival style building as a "blot on the landscape."[4] City Hall offices remained in the building until 1965, when the structure was demolished for urban renewal. Municipal offices moved into the former New York State Electric and Gas Corporation building at 108 East Green Street, erected in 1939. Part of the Seneca Street parking ramp, erected in 1974, now occupies the site of the old City Hall. The loss of this stately structure spurred the formation of Historic Ithaca, a non-profit group dedicated to the preservation of Tompkins County's architectural heritage.

(c. 1910)

(c. 1915)

(1983)

Southwest Corner of State and Tioga Streets

WITH THE HOPES of establishing Ithaca as a prominent theatre town, brothers Henry L. and John M. Wilgus constructed a hall, large enough to seat 1,000 people, on the third floor of their building located at the southwest corner of State and Tioga Streets. The Wilgus Block, erected in 1868 at a cost of $60,000, was designed by Buffalo architects Wilcox and Porter, the firm responsible for Morrill Hall on the Cornell campus. Officially named the Atheneum, the theatre was dubbed the Wilgus Opera House by local residents. The dry goods stores of the Wilgus Brothers and later the firm of Marsh and Hall occupied the ground floor until 1889, when Jacob Rothschild moved his Boston Variety Store from the northwest corner of State and Aurora Streets into the building. His two brothers, Isaac and Daniel, joined him in the business soon thereafter. After the Opera House closed, the theatre was leased to the Ithaca Conservatory of Music. When the *Ithaca Journal* moved from their offices on South Tioga Street into the Titus Block on West State Street in 1905, the Rothschild brothers purchased and remodelled the building to hold their expanding business. Next to the Wilgus Block at 149 East State Street stood the Sprague Block, designed by Alfred B. Dale, and built by Joseph Brittin Sprague in 1871. When this photograph was taken the second floor of the building housed William Wykoff's Phonographic Institute, a School of Stenography and Typewriting, founded in

1876, and one of the first business schools in the United States. The Andrus Block at 141 East State Street contained the prosperous firm of Andrus and Church, long established printers and dealers in books and stationery. In 1913-14 the Rothschild brothers launched a major renovation of the Wilgus Block. The building was stripped of its exterior walls and roof and a new facade was added, designed by local architects Gibb and Waltz.

UNDERTAKING ANOTHER major expansion in 1974, the firm constructed a new structure at the southwest corner of State and Aurora Streets. The former Rothschild's Department Store and the Sprague and Journal Blocks were demolished that year to clear land for the revitalization of downtown. Work began soon thereafter on the construction of a two-block pedestrian mall on State Street between Cayuga and Aurora Streets. Tioga Street between State and Green Streets was permanently closed. State Street was transformed with a variety of trees, play areas, covered pavilions and a fountain. The Ithaca Commons was designed by Anton J. Egner and Associates, architects, and Marvin Adleman, landscape architect. In 1980 construction of Center Ithaca began on the former Rothschild's site. The multi-use building by Werner Seligman and Associates of Cortland, New York, features shops, offices and apartments.

In 1905 twelve clothing stores were located on the two blocks of East State Street between Cayuga and Aurora Streets. At the time this photograph was taken, the entire clothing stock of Philip Seamon's store at 150 East State Street had been placed in the hands of the McGill Mercantile Company of Chicago, buyers of bankrupt, assignee and salvage stocks. The company utilized an eye-catching mode of advertising: a painted sign extending two full stories announced a special ten day sale beginning on April 8. Men's clothing was offered well below cost, including fine dress pants for 98 cents, overcoats for $2.98, suits made of vicunas, cheviot, worsteds or wire twist tweeds for $6.98 and silk embroidered suspenders for six cents. Seamon's brother Barney operated a clothing shop in the building to the left, and Charles H. Brooks ran a jewelry store in the building to the right.

150 East State Street (1905)

THE CLOTHING SHOP of Baxter and Burris replaced Seamon's store by 1909. The building housed various mercantile businesses until 1970, when a restaurant opened in the ground floor. People's Pottery now occupies the building. While their upper stories remain largely the same, all three buildings have received new storefronts since the 1905 view was taken. The Carrara glass storefront of Schooley's Jewelry at 152 East State Street is one of the few extant Art Deco style storefronts in the city.

150 The Commons

Southeast Corner of State and Cayuga Streets (1910-1916)

TREMAN, KING AND COMPANY occupied this site at the southeast corner of State and Cayuga Streets for 95 years. Brothers Leonard and Lafayette Treman purchased the hardware holdings of E. G. Pelton in 1844 and immediately opened for business. In 1857 Leander R. King, a cousin, was admitted to the firm, and the name changed to Treman, King and Company. Throughout the nineteenth and early twentieth centuries the company supplied the needs of the growing community, living up to the spirit of their slogan, "Truth only; Facts always." Patronage increased steadily until 1878 when larger quarters were needed and this four-story brick building was erected. An advertisement in 1891 indicated the store stocked "a complete line of hardware, mechanical tools, shelf goods, house furnishing goods, and tinware of every description, several styles of stoves and ranges, paints, oils, all kinds of glass, bar iron and steel and many other specialities too numerous to mention."[5]

Next door on State Street stood the original Bank of Ithaca building, a monumental Greek Revival style structure with a portico and six columns, erected in 1829. With two of its columns removed to provide entries to the ground floor, the building housed a number of retail establishments after the bank's closing in 1850. The Post Office occupied the building from 1882 until its present quarters at East Buffalo and North Tioga Streets were completed in 1909. Atwater's Grocery and Bakery moved in immediately thereafter. Under their ownership the structure was first referred to as the "Colonial Building."

Around the corner at 113 South Cayuga Street stood the Lyceum Theatre, erected in 1893 and designed with a porticoed front by theatrical architect Leon H. Lempert from Rochester. After its first performance, "Il Trovatore" by Verdi, the Lyceum presented a new play every second or third night, ranging from slapstick comedy to productions of Shakespeare. The theatre became established as a tryout center for New York City shows, hosting performances by John Barrymore, Sarah Bernhart and Lillian Russell.

Southeast Corner of State and Cayuga Streets

TWICE BESET BY FIRE in the first decade of the twentieth century the Treman, King and Company Building was engulfed by flames and completely destroyed on May 4, 1921. A new building, designed by Gibb and Waltz, was erected by the company in 1922. Treman, King and Company closed their doors in 1939, bringing to an end one of the oldest family-run businesses in Ithaca. Montgomery Ward then occupied the building for almost three decades. In 1934 Atwater's truncated the distinctive colonnaded front of the Colonial Building to extend their storefront. The Lyceum Theatre, unable to compete with the growing popularity of motion pictures, was demolished in 1933.

Cayuga Street, Looking South Toward Green Street (1907)

EIGHT VOLUNTEER fire departments marched through the streets of downtown Ithaca on Firemen's Day, September 12, 1907. This view, looking south onto Cayuga Street from atop the portico of the Lyceum Theatre, captures the procession of the Protective Police leading the parade. Prominent citizens, including architect Clinton Vivian, former Mayor Henry A. St. John (1891-2), and businessmen Robert H. Treman and Edward G. Wyckoff, all dressed in frock coats and carrying opera hats and canes, were among the marchers.

When this photograph was taken, George Baker's meat market and John Leonard's grocery occupied the corner building at 126-128 South Cayuga Street. This three-story brick veneered structure with a projecting wooden bay was built in 1885. The small one-and-one-half-story Greek Revival style residence across the street was built by 1850 and was the early home of Benjamin A. Atwater. The next building to the south housed both the Ithaca Automobile Company and McClune's Bicycle Exchange.

Cayuga Street, Looking South Toward Green Street

THE LYCEUM THEATRE and its portico no longer stand, but a similar view is seen in this photograph taken from the third floor of the neighboring Jamieson and McKinney Block. Cayuga Street south of Green Street has radically changed. The Greek Revival house was demolished in the early 1920's, replaced by an automobile service center by 1925. By the late 1960's the remaining block had been cleared for urban renewal, and the Ramada Inn was erected in 1973. The building at 126-128 South Cayuga Street, missing its balconette but its wooden bay intact, now houses a bar and liquor store.

110-112 West Green Street (1916)

THIS GARAGE at 110-112 West Green Street was erected in 1915 to house the Cole Garage Company, operated by Walter W. Cole. As is pictured in this photograph, the Company sold the latest Mitchell and Chevrolet models. The second car from the left, a "Chevrolet Four-Ninety," sold for $490 in 1916. The second car from the right is a brand new 1917 Chevrolet. Six other garages were in operation in the city at that time; Cole's nearest neighbor was the Lang Garage on the next block east on Green Street.

110-112 West Green Street

VARIOUS OTHER garages were located here until the mid-1940's. The Townsend Manufacturing and Tool Corporation, makers of precision machine work, occupied the structure until 1970 when Ithaca Photo moved in. The buildings next door to the left were torn down in 1949 to make way for the expansion of the *Ithaca Journal* plant.

State Street Looking West from Cayuga Street (1905-1912)

Although State Street east of Cayuga was Ithaca's commercial center when this photograph was taken, the 100 block of West State Street contained numerous long-standing businesses as well as a few of Ithaca's earliest commercial structures. In the center of the south side of the block stood the Bank of Newburgh Building with a distinctive pilastered facade, erected circa 1821 to house a branch of the Hudson River concern. In 1829 the bank merged with the Bank of Ithaca, and its operations were relocated to the Colonial Building on East State Street. John L. Whiton, operator of a steam bakery shown to the left of the building at 107 West State Street, lived in the bank building for 40 years. For over two decades the buildings at 103 and 105 West State Street contained a furniture dealer and a bakery, respectively. At the time of this photograph the Office Hotel had just opened, replacing the grocery run by Richard Crozier and various partners. Across the street on the corner stood the Hibbard Block, erected in 1847 to house the general merchandise and variety store of H. F. Hibbard. Before the Hibbard Block the Columbian Inn occupied the corner lot. The Inn was perhaps most famous as the site of the first recorded murder in the village of Ithaca in 1831.

State Street Looking West from Cayuga Street

THOUGH SLATED for demolition in 1912, the Bank of Newburgh building was moved to the lot at 106 East Court Street, where it serves as a residence and offices today. By 1917 the Security Garage, operated by the Bovard Brothers, was erected on the bank site and the adjoining vacant lot. Though much of the garage storefront remains the same, a marquee and ticket booth entrance were added in 1928 when the building was transformed into the State Street Theatre. The movie *Show Girl* and live entertainment comprised the opening night program on December 6, 1928. The State was Ithaca's first "semi-atmospheric" theatre, according to the architect, Victor A. Rigaumont. The theatre, capable of seating 1,818 persons, also contained 32 drop sets for vaudeville acts, a $26,000 organ, eight dressing rooms, and two projection machines. A new three-story building housing the Chanticleer tap room was built on the site of the Crozier block in 1947. The Chanticleer's distinctive neon rooster has been designated an historic sign by the city.

Exchange Hotel, 122 West State Street (1900)

LITTLE IS KNOWN of the early days of the Exchange Hotel, located at 122 West State Street, although the structure could easily be the second oldest hotel extant in Ithaca after the Clinton House. The hotel was managed after 1849 by Edmund H. Watkins, who had arrived in Ithaca twenty-four years earlier to operate a stage on the Catskill Turnpike. In 1875 the hotel was advertised as "a strictly temperance house."6 Joseph LaPoint, who had managed a blacksmith shop in a building on the neighboring site at 128 West State Street, became proprietor of the Exchange Hotel in 1890. As shown in this photograph, LaPoint hung a Welcome sign over the door of his saloon on September 20, 1900, the day the Ithaca Fire Department held its annual parade and inspection. The Excelsior Engine Company and Band from Trumansburg were that year's guests of the Department. As with every annual firefighter's parade, the residents of the city responded by festooning many of the commercial buildings along the procession with bright decorations, flags, and bunting to show their appreciation for the service these men provided.

State Street Smoke Shop, 124 West State Street

THE DOORS of the Exchange Hotel closed around 1928. Significant storefront and floor level changes were made mid-century. Many different retail businesses leased space on the ground floor while the top floors were used for rental apartments. The current occupant, the State Street Smoke Shop, entered the building in 1971.

Titus and Stowell Block, 123-131 West State Street (1905-1907)

JOHN C. STOWELL came to Ithaca from Groton in 1835 to work in a general store. In 1872 he and his son Calvin began a wholesale grocery and produce business at 135 West State Street, a small three-story brick building shown at the right of this photograph, that had previously been occupied by J. H. Hintermister, an organ manufacturer. Soon they needed larger quarters. Together with Charles Titus, the real estate entrepreneur, Messrs. Stowell & Son built the larger four-story French Second Empire style brick block next door in 1876 to house their expanding business. The building, known as the Titus and Stowell Block, was designed by Alfred B. Dale. From 1901-1907 the upper floors were occupied by the YMCA, and contained social and reading rooms, a gymnasium, shower baths, and bowling alleys for use by members. In 1905 the *Ithaca Journal* moved into the building from their previous headquarters in the Journal Block located on South Tioga Street.

In 1901 the New York and Pennsylvania Telephone and Telegraph Company built the neighboring building at 121 West State for use as a telephone exchange. Telephone service was offered in Ithaca as early as 1878 due to the successful experiments pioneered by physics professor William A. Anthony of Cornell University. The first telephone company, formed by Anthony and Captain William O. Wyckoff, was sold in 1883 to the New York and Pennsylvania Telephone and Telegraph Company. The buff brick single-story building designed by Clinton L. Vivian was perhaps Ithaca's first building of "fireproof" construction, built with a cast concrete steel floor system.

The Ithaca Journal Building, 123 West State Street

TODAY TREES obscure an identical view and the current photograph must be taken from the street. The New York Telephone building appears much larger than in the historic view. The *Ithaca Journal* made numerous alterations to the Titus and Stowell Block. In the early 1950's the two top stories were removed, and later a new brick and plate glass facade was added. It is difficult to picture an earlier building behind the present stark facade, but the nineteenth century brickwork with segmental arches remains visible along the eastern wall, adjacent to the alleyway. In 1909 the New York Telephone Company obtained control of the New York and Pennsylvania Telephone and Telegraph Company and continued to operate from the West State Street exchange. Another company, the Federal Telephone and Telegraph Company located opposite the Post Office, was also absorbed into the Bell system. The two exchanges operated separately until 1921 when service in Ithaca was consolidated in the Tioga Street exchange. For almost three decades the Salvation Army operated out of the State Street structure. Today an architectural consultant and a printing establishment occupy the building.

East Side of Geneva Street Looking North from State Street (c.1866)

By THE END of the nineteenth century eight religious denominations were organized in Ithaca: Presbyterian, Baptist, Roman Catholic, Congregational, Episcopal, Methodist, Free Methodist and Unitarian. This photograph of North Geneva Street towards Seneca Street presents a rare view of three neighboring places of worship. The parish of the Catholic Church formed in 1848 during a time of Irish immigration into the city. In 1851 the small two-story Greek Revival style structure in the center of this photograph was erected and dedicated as St. Luke's. The parish soon outgrew this building and in 1860 a new church, the Immaculate Conception of the Blessed Virgin, was erected just north of the small structure at the southwest corner of Seneca and Geneva Streets. The earlier church building was then used as the parsonage. The colonnaded church fronting Seneca Street, partially hidden on the left, was erected by the Protestant Reformed Dutch Church in 1830. The two-story residence in the foreground, erected shortly before this photograph was taken, was the home of Richard A. Crozier, who operated a grocery store at 101 West State Street.

East Side of Geneva Street Looking North from State Street

IN 1872 the members of the Dutch Reformed Church voted to sever their ties with their parent organization to become a congregational church. On November 14, 1874, Charles Tyler was installed as the first pastor of the newly formed First Church of Christ. Under Tyler's direction the wooden structure was replaced by the present brick building, designed by Ithaca architect William Henry Miller. In 1966 the church was purchased by the St. Catherine Greek Orthodox Church. By 1883 the first Catholic Church structure had been moved to 611 West Green Street where it stands today, and a new parsonage erected. The third and present Catholic Church was designed by A. B. Wood and erected in 1894. To clear the site for the new building, the second church was moved to the rear of the lot. It was demolished in 1976.

(c.1870)

(c.1880)

(1983)

Clinton House, 116-120 North Cayuga Street

FOLLOWING ITS OPENING on June 3, 1830, the Clinton House was hailed as one of the finest hotels west of the Hudson River. Built by businessmen Jeremiah Beebe, Henry Ackley and Henry Hibbard, the hotel was named in honor of DeWitt Clinton, Governor of New York from 1817 to 1822 and 1824 to 1828. The monumental Greek Revival style building boasted 150 rooms, an audacious project considering Ithaca's population was less than 4,000 at the time. The Clinton House served as an important center for political and social events. Village Council meetings were held there until 1843, and the Whig and Democratic parties located their campaign headquarters in the building. In 1864 the hotel underwent extensive interior renovation. A new roof, designed by William Henry Miller in the then-popular French Second Empire style, was added in 1872.

ON MARCH 23, 1901, a major fire completely destroyed the top floor and roof, while the lower floors were heavily damaged by water and falling debris. Local architect Clinton L. Vivian, commissioned to provide plans for rebuilding the hotel, designed a new roof with a sheet metal balustrade in a style similar to its original classicial form. The building continued to serve as a hotel until 1972, though it began to deteriorate with advancing age. Purchased that year by Historic Ithaca, the Clinton House was remade into an office building, with the ground floor and basement housing the DeWitt Historical Society of Tompkins County. The restoration was a popular community project with volunteers providing much of the labor. Today Ithaca's most prominent landmark serves as an example of successful adaptive reuse.

Ithaca High School, Northeast Corner of Cayuga and Seneca Streets (1900-1912)

ITHACA'S FIRST SCHOOL was erected on this site in 1807. Twelve years later construction of a private school, the Ithaca Academy, began. In 1874 a state law established a system of graded schools in the Village of Ithaca under the control of a Board of Education. Grammar and high school classes were then held in the Academy building until 1884 when that structure was demolished. In the same year it was replaced by the high school designed by architect A. B. Wood, shown in this photograph. Grammar school classes were held on the first story and high school classes on the second. In 1887 high school students had the choice of four courses of study leading to a diploma: Academic, Classical, English and Commercial. An eleventh year student in the Academic course was required to study plane geometry, elementary physics, civil government and the history of Rome, with electives in German, French, history of Greece, Virgil's Aeneid, geology, solid geometry and advanced physics. The high school building soon proved to be too small and a four-room annex on Seneca Street was built in 1892. Eight years later an annex facing Buffalo Street was added.

The DeWitt Mall, Northeast Corner of Cayuga and Seneca Streets

ON FEBRUARY 12, 1912 the high school was destroyed by fire. Emergency classroom accommodations were secured in nearby residences on Seneca and Buffalo Streets as well as in the Elks Lodge at the corner of State and Geneva Streets. Construction of the new high school began immediately under the supervision of architect William Henry Miller. Grammar and high school classes resumed in the building in June of 1914. After the high school moved into a new complex erected on Percy Field near Fall Creek in 1960, this building housed the DeWitt Junior High School. Eleven years later when a new junior high school was erected adjacent to the Fall Creek site, the structure was sold at public auction. Converted by architect William Downing into the DeWitt Mall, the former school houses apartments, offices and shops.

Star Theatre, 118-120 East Seneca Street (1911)

BY THE END of the first decade of the twentieth century Ithaca boasted of nine theatres, most featuring vaudeville acts and the latest form of entertainment, motion pictures. The original Star Theatre was built at the southwest corner of Green and Tioga Streets in 1908. Just two years later it had outgrown its 467-seat capacity, and was sold to become the Billiken Movie House. In 1911 construction began for the New Star Theatre at 118-120 East Seneca Street, following the demolition of a nineteenth century residence previously on the site. The new theatre, shown with its construction crew in front, was designed by the Ithaca firm of Gibb and Waltz and seated 1200 people. On opening night, September 18, 1911, the theatre presented "the great Wallace MacKay, musical mimic, the Four Charles, European Comedy Novelty"[7] and selected motion pictures to a standing-room-only audience. There were three vaudeville acts daily, at 3:30 p.m., 7:00 p.m., and 9:30 p.m., with admission at 15 cents for a seat in the orchestra.

Tompkins County Trust Company Drive-In, 118-120 East Seneca Street

THE NEW STAR THEATRE became Ithaca's most popular vaudeville house and gained recognition as a trial house for movies filmed by the local Wharton Studios between 1914 and 1919. In 1920 the Star Theatre merged with the Crescent and the Strand Theatres and its doors closed. Ithaca College, then the Ithaca Conservatory of Music, bought the property in 1921 for use as a physical education facility. When Ithaca College moved to its new South Hill campus in 1966, the building was transferred to the Tompkins County Trust Company and demolished to create additional parking for the bank. In 1977 a drive-in banking facility was erected.

119-121 East Buffalo Street (1913)

ON APRIL 25, 1912, Central Elementary School, located on the southwest corner of Court and Albany Streets, burned to the ground, only two months after the high school had been destroyed by fire. Superintendent of Schools David Henry Boynton appealed to the community for the use of downtown residences to house temporarily classes for the 500 displaced Central School students and their teachers. As a result, Central students were divided among several buildings downtown. This residence at 119-121 East Buffalo Street, occupied by Frederick W. Phillips, an insurance agent, and Dr. Arthur D. White, was offered to the school. At the time of this photograph the western half of the building housed kindergarten and first and second grades. For one year the Board of Education maintained an office in the eastern half. Constructed originally as two joined townhouses with distinctive stepped gable end walls, the building may date from the late 1840's.

119-121 East Buffalo Street

THE ARCHITECT'S PLANS for the new high school were modified slightly to accommodate the displaced elementary school students. The Phillps Annex was used for only two years and by June 1914 classes resumed in the adjacent new high school. The building again served as a residence until the 1960's. A travel agency, an architect's office, and a feminist bookstore, Smedley's, presently occupy the building.

ON THE SOUTHEAST corner of Buffalo and Tioga Streets, at the left of this photograph, in the shade of tall trees, stood the Greek Revival style residence of Henry Hibbard, built in 1819. The wedding ceremony for Henry's daughter Mary and Thomas P. St. John took place in this home in 1839; after Hibbard's death in 1863 it became the St. John residence. Thomas P. St. John was the first cashier for the Bank of Ithaca between 1829 and 1833, and later manufactured sewing silks with his brother-in-law, Henry Fitch Hibbard. Thomas was elected President of the Village in 1859. The St. Johns raised five children; their son Henry A. St. John was mayor of Ithaca in 1891-92. Mary remained in the house after her husband's death in 1880. She died in 1896 and the house was sold to Edward G. and Charles F. Wyckoff. At the time this photograph was taken this block of North Tioga was still a quiet residential street.

IN 1898 the St. John house was moved to the rear of the lot to face Buffalo Street and was given a brick veneer. The Federal Government purchased the corner lot in 1903 for the site of the new Post Office and the building was moved again, to 411 West Seneca Street. In 1908-09 the Post Office was constructed, to a design by federal architect James Knox Taylor. The Italianate style residence on the corner was demolished in 1954 and replaced by a second expansion of the New York Telephone building, originally built for the Federal Telephone and Telegraph Company around 1912.

South Side of Buffalo Street
at Tioga Street

YMCA, Northeast Corner of Buffalo
and Tioga Streets (c.1920)

THE FIRST RECORDED meeting of the Young Men's Christian Association in Ithaca was held on November 23, 1868, in the reading room of the Cornell Library on Tioga Street. By the end of the century the "Y" broadened its programs from a distinctly religious emphasis to a "three-point program for the spirit, mind and body"[8] and hosted lectures, evening educational classes, and a physical education program in addition to religious meetings. The YMCA rented space in the Cornell Library until its move in 1887 to a building on the northwest corner of Seneca and Tioga Streets where a gymnasium and shower baths were installed. In 1901 the organization moved to the upper floors of the Titus and Stowell Block on West State Street.

Undertaking a major expansion in 1907 the "Y" purchased from Miss Mary E. Humphrey a house and a lot at the northeast corner of Buffalo and Tioga Streets. As was common with residences that stood in the way of Ithaca's brisk commercial expansion at the turn of the century, the building was sold and moved. Using a portable tramway to winch the building down Buffalo Street, L. S. Bagley set it on his lot at the corner of Cascadilla and Meadow Streets. The new YMCA building, designed by Gibb and Waltz, opened on October 12, 1908. It contained offices on the first floor, a kitchen and dining room on the second, and dormitories for men on the third and fourth floors.

Northeast Corner of Buffalo and Tioga Streets

THE "Y" BUILDING succumbed to arson on May 13, 1978 and was consequently demolished. The present office building replaced it in April of 1983. Designed by Ithaca architect David Taube, the new building's west basement wall features a line of tiles from the old "Y's" swimming pool. The YMCA recently erected a new facility in the Town of Lansing.

Wood Street from South Hill (c.1890)

MOST OF THE LAND south of Six Mile Creek in the southern flats of Ithaca remained completely undeveloped for residential use until the early 1890's. Charles M. Titus, primary owner of the area, planned the development of the land as early as 1869. A map of his holdings dated February 1, 1869 shows a plan for extending Albany, Plain and Corn Streets south of Clinton Street and subdividing the resulting blocks into parcels for future sale. The marshy land needed many improvements before development could occur. To control the occasional flooding of Six Mile Creek a new channel was built along Titus Avenue in the late 1870's. By the early 1880's a few houses had been built on Spencer Place west of Tioga Street. Soon thereafter Titus and Fred Marsh erected a number of houses on the South Geneva and South Albany Street extensions. One of the first was a spired residence visible here at the corner of Wood and South Albany Streets, erected about 1885. Wood Street, the first east-west extension from Albany Street south of Six Mile Creek, ended abruptly in the haystacks of a farmer's field. Due west of Meadow Street stood the Tompkins County Agricultural and Horticultural Society fairgrounds which relocated here in 1874 from the fairgrounds at Dey and Adams Streets.

Wood Street from South Hill

TODAY SOUTH HILL trees block the identical view, forcing the photographer to a point higher up the hill. This shot, taken from the roof of Morse Chain's plant, still shows the Wood Street house in the lower right foreground, though the corner residence now lacks its distinctive spire. Residential development of the Titus Flats area occurred on a large scale in the first decade of the twentieth century. By 1908 about forty homes had been built. Even as late as the mid-1940's South, Wood, and Park Streets did not extend to Meadow Street. The Tompkins County Agricultural and Horticultural Society held an annual fair at the fairgrounds on Meadow Street until the early 1960's. Construction of New York State Route 13 in 1964 spurred commercial development of the area. Today this southside thoroughfare is lined with supermarkets, fast food restaurants and car dealerships.

Sprague House, Northwest Corner of Titus Avenue and Albany Street (c.1875)

THE SPRAGUE HOUSE at the northwest corner of Titus Avenue and Albany Streets, is one of the most notable of the nineteenth century residences in Ithaca, but few know its significant role in Ithaca's southside history. Most of the land in the City of Ithaca south of Clinton Street was purchased by Charles M. Titus in 1868. Over the next twenty years Titus devoted much of his energies to developing these 400 acres of the original Bloodgood tract, then mostly hillside and marsh. He "ditched, drained and otherwise greatly improved" these lands, and shortly thereafter "laid out that beautiful roadway known as 'Titus Avenue,' which he located, built and bordered with trees."[9] This Second Empire style residence with adjoining carriage house was built for Titus in 1870 from plans by architect Alfred B. Dale. Ironical-ly Titus never occupied the house, but in 1871 swapped the stately residence for a farm in Ohio owned by the husband of his wife's sister, Joseph Brittin Sprague. At that time the Sprague house stood quite alone, its nearest neighbor on Clinton near Geneva Street. Though he was a resident of the city for only seven years until his death in 1878, "Colonel" Sprague was one of Ithaca's most popular and influential citizens. As president of the village in 1877 Sprague was responsible for abolishing free grazing rights for the "poorman's cow" in the streets of Ithaca. In his obituary the *Ithaca Journal* reported, "No death except possibly that of Ezra Cornell's was in many years, if ever, so deeply lamented by the entire community."[10]

Sprague House, Northwest Corner of Titus Avenue and Albany Street

LATE IN THE 1890's Sprague's wife Louisa commissioned a major addition to the mansion. To the north a two-story wing and a three-story pyramidal tower were built and along the north and south facades two porches were added. After her death in 1905 the house was left in trust for St. John's Episcopal Church, and sold two years later. By 1917 the adjoining carriage house had been destroyed by fire and much of the surrounding land sold for residential development. Today the building is subdivided into ten rental apartments.

A.M.E. Zion Church,
116 Cleveland Avenue
(1898-1904)

THROUGHOUT the twentieth century A.M.E. Zion has remained a spiritual as well as secular center for Ithaca's Black community. In 1913 a group of seven students met in the church basement and founded Alpha Phi Alpha, the national Black fraternity. A rose window was added in 1945, dedicated to the church's World War II servicemen. The recent exterior rehabilitation of the church was completed in 1981. The building has been placed on the National Register of Historic Places in recognition of its significance in New York State Black history.

A.M.E. Zion Church,
116 Cleveland Avenue

Northeast Corner of State and Albany Streets (c.1873)

THIS BUILDING, with its prominent arcade and stepped gable ends, was constructed about 1840 to house the Merchants' and Farmers' Bank, located at 214-218 West State Street at the northeast corner of Albany Street. The bank was organized in 1838 by three brothers, Timothy S., Manwell R., and Josiah B. Williams, who were first attracted to central New York by the opening of the Erie Canal. The eastern half of the building was used for the bank, and the western half for a retail establishment selling building supplies, grains, produce, and general merchandise. Josiah acted as president of the bank after the death of his two brothers.

In 1873 the bank merged with the First National Bank of Ithaca and its sign was taken down; it has been removed when this photograph was taken. In 1868 the Ithaca Calendar Clock Company moved from a one room operation at 120 South Cayuga Street to the western portion of this building. They remained until 1874 when their new factory at Dey and Adams Streets, on the former site of the Tompkins County Agricultural and Horticultural Society Fairgrounds, was completed. The Second Empire style residence to the right of the brick block, constructed by Calvin Gardner, had just been built when this photograph was taken.

Northeast Corner of State and Albany Streets

BY 1883 a third story had been added to the structure and a building housed a button factory and a tinsmith shop. At the turn of the century a baker and a meat market occupied the space. Many Ithacans may remember shopping in the various supermarkets that occupied the building from about 1940 until 1958. The brick block was demolished in 1964 and the present building erected soon thereafter.

North Side of State Street Looking West Toward Meadow Street (1905)

ITHACA'S HISTORY is replete with accounts of spring flooding of "The Flats." Besides causing loss of life and property, the recurrent flooding posed a serious health hazard to the Ithaca community and inhibited development near the Inlet. A severe storm on June 21, 1905 brought five inches of rain in ten hours, seriously flooding the West End. As the flood waters receded children played in the inundated streets. In this view along West State Street, billboards plastered with advertisements partially screen the vacant lots at Meadow Street between State and Seneca, which had remained undeveloped through the nineteenth century.

North Side of State Street Looking West Toward Meadow Street

PUBLIC WORKS along Six Mile Creek in 1906-08 alleviated the threat of flooding on "The Flats" and made the area more secure for development. By 1930 the vacant West State Street lots had been sold and a row of commercial establishments built, including a gasoline station, shoe repair, barber shop and granite and marble works. The connection of Meadow Street to New York State Route 13 in 1964 revitalized commercial development of the area. Lower State Street remains a main thoroughfare between downtown and the West End. This block of West State Street is part of the City's current street improvement program.

D. L. and W. Railroad Station, 710 West State Street (c.1919)

THE ITHACA BRANCH of the Delaware, Lackawanna and Western Railroad was one of the company's principal routes on the "Road of Anthracite." The D. L. and W. acquired the Cayuga and Susquehanna Railroad, successor to the Ithaca and Owego Railroad, in 1849. The railroad carried northern Pennsylvania anthracite coal to the shores of Cayuga Lake, where it was transferred to waiting barges for delivery to ports further north. Though by the end of the century the railroad derived a large percentage of its revenue from the transportation of coal and other freight, the company provided passenger service as well. Ithaca was excluded from the company's main lines due to the hilly terrain, but three passenger trains to Owego enabled the travelling Ithacan to connect to the "Phoebe Snow" to New York City. The company erected a new passenger depot around 1919 below West Seneca Street near Fulton Street, replacing an earlier wooden structure. The brick station, pictured in this photograph, is decorated with glazed ceramic tiles and is similar to other D. L. and W. depots in the region.

Greyhound Bus Station, 710 West State Street

THE D. L. AND W. discontinued passenger service through Ithaca in 1942. Freight service was suspended fourteen years later. The station was rented to various concerns until 1967 when it was purchased by Greyhound Bus Lines. Still a depot for travellers, the building retains many interior features from its railroad days. The Tompkins County Trust Company branch office in the rear, built in 1966, mirrors the station's design. The commercial structure in the foreground, built eight years earlier, now houses a doughnut shop.

Intersection of Buffalo and Westport Streets Looking Northwest (c.1900)

ITHACA ENTERED the age of locomotives in 1828 with the Ithaca and Owego Railroad, the second line chartered in the state. Even as late as the end of the Civil War, only one railroad, the Delaware, Lackawanna, and Western, served Ithaca. However, by 1883 four railways and a steamboat line passed through town. Most of these lines were incorporated into the Lehigh Valley system by the turn of the century. The Ithaca branch of the Lehigh Valley Railroad was a profitable passenger route for the company. Service of the Black Diamond Express, the deluxe train running between New York and Buffalo, began in 1896, and passed through Ithaca daily. In 1898 the company erected a new passenger terminal on Buffalo Street near Brindley Street on the site of their previous depot. The terminal was designed by local architect A. B. Wood, who was responsible for the design of other Lehigh Valley depots.

The West End experienced a surge of development when the railroad company located their first depot there in the late 1870's. Many hotels that catered to canal and railroad workers as well as to travelers were built near the depot. The three-story wood frame structure in the foreground is the Lehigh Valley House, erected in 1878 for William Seaman. The building was designed by architect Alfred B. Dale. Shown in the background of this photograph is Patten's Hotel, the two-story building with a cast-iron balconette, that was erected the same year. At the time this photograph was taken the trolley passed by every ten minutes.

Intersection of Buffalo and Taughannock Boulevard Looking Northwest

IN THE TWENTIETH century the Lehigh Valley company ran popular excursions such as the "Big Red Special" to and from New York, as well as "Honeymoon Express" trains to Niagara Falls. Passenger traffic dwindled as bus and automobile travel became more convenient. Passenger service to Ithaca was discontinued on February 4, 1961. The depot stood vacant until 1966 when the structure was converted into the Station Restaurant. Of the two hotels, only the Lehigh Valley House remains in operation.

Brindley Street, Looking South from Buffalo Street (c.1905)

IN THE EARLY nineteenth century coal and boat yards were the only activities in the West End, but they were soon supplanted by a few manufacturing concerns that located adjacent to the Cayuga Inlet. By the beginning of the twentieth century the area had become a major industrial center for Ithaca as well as a transshipping point for the region. The area shown in this photograph, taken from the Lehigh Valley Railroad depot, is the intersection of Brindley, West Seneca and West State Streets at the junction of the Inlet and Six Mile Creek. Visible on the right is the Ithaca Sign Works building, originally constructed in 1877 for the Ithaca Organ and Piano Company, manufacturers of five-octave and six-octave reed organs. In 1900 Ogilvie Stanford and William H. Crowell, manufacturers of advertising novelties and signs, moved their business into this brick building. Just visible behind the Sign Works building is a warehouse of the Cornell Incubator Company. The large barn located across the tracks was used by Robinson and Carpenter, a lumber and building supplies company, that opened at that location in 1887. The railroad crossing sign in the foreground warns the passerby to "stop and listen, look out for the cars."

Looking South from Buffalo Street

THE TRACKS reaching to the depot were removed during the construction of the flood control channel at the Inlet in 1968. At that time Brindley Street was closed to traffic and West Seneca Street was rerouted. The Sign Works remained in the brick warehouse until 1942 when Cooperative GLF Exchange, Inc., a predecessor to Agway, bought the building. McPherson Sailing Products acquired the structure in 1967 for the manufacture of sailboats. The building will soon be renovated for office space. In 1914 the Cornell Incubator Company holdings were purchased by William T. Thomas, manager of the Thomas Brothers Aeroplane Company of Bath, New York. During World War I the plant operated around the clock producing aircraft. The lumber sheds were recently removed to make way for a car wash. A salvaged railroad crossing sign, visible in the foreground, is one of the few reminders of the West End's importance as an industrial center.

Cascadilla Cove (c.1900)

CASCADILLA CREEK begins seven miles east of Ithaca, running from Ellis Hollow to the head of Cayuga Lake. Its name may derive from the Spanish word for "little cascade," a fitting appellation for a creek which descends from above Cornell to Cayuga Lake without a major waterfall. Ithaca's first white residents settled by the Creek at the base of East Hill. Though the first mill in Tompkins County was established on Cascadilla ravine around 1790-1800 by Jacob Yaple,

Cascadilla Creek never became the major industrial center that Fall Creek was by the turn of the twentieth century. In 1851 the Creek was straightened and directed through an "avenue of willows" running northwest from Cayuga Street to the lake. The junction of the Creek with the Inlet was known as Cascadilla Cove. The north bank was lined with wooden boathouses which served the anglers who frequented the lake.

Cascadilla Cove

THE BOATHOUSES along Cascadilla Creek were all demolished by the early 1960's. Today the Cove is the site of Johnson's Boat Yard. Established by Frederick E. Johnson in 1913, the business is one of several marine supply houses serving the recreational boat owners who sail and motor on Cayuga Lake.

On JUNE 14, 1818 the first boat passed through the newly constructed locks at Seneca Falls, signalling the beginning of an era of canal barge traffic on Cayuga Lake. The Cayuga Inlet was partially navigable at that time, and boats travelling from the Erie Canal brought supplies into Ithaca. The Inlet was declared a public highway in 1821, the same year in which the Village was incorporated. Sand bars that obstructed the channel were removed, and by the late 1820's lake steamers that had originally docked at Port Renwick at the end of the lake landed in a port on the Inlet. A state-owned pier, 1,550 feet in length, was built at the mouth of the Inlet in 1838. In 1889, shortly before this photograph was taken, the pier was rebuilt. The lighthouse appears to predate the pier, judging from its design and the graffiti inscribed on its wooden base. At that time the spot appears to have been popular with local anglers.

Cayuga Inlet Lighthouse
(c.1898)

THE 1899 annual report of the New York State Engineer and Surveyor stated that a new lighthouse of steel construction had been erected on Cayuga Lake, replacing a deteriorated wooden structure. The lighthouse, now lacking its original protective metal top, enabled boats to enter the harbor at night. Though by the turn of the century canal boat shipping had been largely supplanted by freight trains, the harbor enjoyed a resurgence of commercial use with the construction of the Barge Canal along the route of the old Erie Canal. The Inlet was widened and deepened, embankments were built along Fall Creek and lower Six Mile Creek, and upper Six Mile Creek was deepened and diked. Canal barge traffic on the Lake had all but ended by 1940, but the Inlet soon saw a resumption of recreational boating. Two major private marinas and a large state facility cater to boat owners on the Inlet. Today only an occasional visitor wanders out on the pier.

Cayuga Inlet Lighthouse

Renwick Park, Looking Southwest from East Shore Drive (1912-1914)

A FRANCHISE granted to the newly created Cayuga Lake Electric Railway Company in 1874 permitted a track to be extended from Railway (now Lincoln) Avenue, to the Lake at Port Renwick. At the same time the railway company purchased a square mile of the original Renwick estate at the head of the Lake, for development of an amusement park. The company immediately erected park buildings and a long pier for use as a steamboat landing. By the end of the summer a bathhouse, an ice-cream parlor, a dancing pavilion and a casino had been completed. Excursions offered by the railroads brought people in from Scranton, Wilkes-Barre, Binghamton, Elmira, Rochester, Cortland, and other nearby towns to enjoy the amusements. Twelve thousand people visited Renwick Park on July 4, 1894. One of the most popular attractions was "Patsy" Conway's Band and Ithaca "overnight became a mecca for pleasure seekers."[11] Eventually the popularity of the park declined, and in 1914 the railway company sold the property to the Renwick Park and Traffic Association. They in turn leased the park to the Wharton Brothers for use as a motion picture studio. The famous serial thriller "The Exploits of Elaine," starring Lionel Barrymore and Pearl White, was filmed at Renwick Park.

Stewart Park, Looking Southwest from East Shore Drive

GUIDED BY Mayor Edwin C. Stewart's interest in Renwick Park, the city purchased and restored the grounds to their former beauty in 1921. The following year Stewart died, leaving a fund of $150,000 for the preservation of the park which was soon renamed in his memory. Due to Stewart's generous trust, the Fuertes Bird Sanctuary, tennis courts, picnic grounds and a golf course were built. One of the original park buildings, the water tower, was destroyed by Hurricane Hazel in 1954. Due to silt build-up and pollution from the nearby sewage treatment plant, swimming was finally banned in 1961. Stewart Park, however, remains one of Ithaca's most popular receational sites.

Fall Creek, Looking West from the Stewart Avenue Bridge (c.1898)

THE LARGE WATERFALL at the base of Fall Creek proved an attractive spot to nineteenth-century entrepreneurs. The falls were developed for hydropower use as early as 1813, when Phineas Bennett erected a plaster and carding mill below the falls. The first Fall Creek grist mill was erected in 1817. At that time water was channelled from above the falls through a wooden flume supported by beams mortised into the face of the gorge. In 1831 twenty-four-year-old Ezra Cornell directed work for mill owner J. S. Beebe, and blasted a 200-foot long and 10-foot by 13-foot tunnel through the steep, rocky sides of Fall Creek gorge. Beyond the tunnel Cornell excavated an open raceway to funnel water to the in-dustries below. The entrance to the tunnel, adjacent to the dam, can be viewed in the lower left-hand corner of this photograph, shot from the Stewart Avenue bridge. By the end of the nineteenth century sprawling complexes of grist mills, paper mills, and the Ithaca Gun Company lined the creek bed below. A small community of mill worker residences developed on the adjacent flats, though much of the area remained undeveloped at the end of the century. The arched iron bridge in the center crossed the creek at Lake Street adjacent to the Fall Creek Milling Company. The stands at Percy Field athletic grounds can be viewed to the right of the bridge.

Fall Creek, Looking West from the Stewart Avenue Bridge

OF ALL THE manufactories that once lined Fall Creek, only Ithaca Gun Company remains. Ithaca High School, constructed on Percy Field in 1960, is visible to the right. The spectacular 120-foot cataract remains one of Ithaca's most beautiful scenic wonders, and the park at the base of the falls serves hikers, picnickers and fishermen. The disused tunnel is dammed at its entrance and now only a small stream trickles through the raceway. Construction of a new hydroelectric plant at the base of the falls has been proposed by the City, and the power of Fall Creek may be tapped once again.

West Side of Eddy Street, Looking North from Buffalo Street (c.1928)

THOUGH NOT as well travelled as College Avenue today, Eddy Street was in the past the most frequently used approach to campus. The street was named after Otis Eddy, owner of a cotton mill erected in 1826 near the site of Cascadilla Hall. The northern end remained relatively undeveloped until late in the century, although the southern end was lined with residences, including the home of local architect William Henry Miller at 122 Eddy Street. By the turn of the century the block between Buffalo and William Streets was lined with shops catering to the student clientele. When this photograph was taken, school supplies were available at the College Book Store, tuxedo rental at Lucas' Clothing Store, and a hot meal at the Lynden Lunch.

West Side of Eddy Street, Looking North from Buffalo Street

A FIRE IN 1968 destroyed the Alt Heidelberg, a popular student "watering hole" at 408-410 Eddy Street, and a fast food restaurant was built on the site. Cabbagetown Cafe replaced the Elba Italian Kitchen at 404 Eddy Street in 1976 when Elba's moved next door. A laundromat now occupies the corner store.

Sheldon Court, 412-420 Heustis Street (c.1905)

BY THE 1880's Heustis Street (now College Avenue) was lined with residences, many of them boarding houses for Cornell students. Lorenzo Scott Heustis was one of the first residents to build on the street, and lived at 307 College Avenue until his death in 1891. The expansion of the city up East Hill to College Avenue in the late nineteenth century was largely due to the development of the electric transit system. The first trolleys ran on December 12, 1887; at that time Ithaca had one of only thirteen electric lines in operation in the country. In 1892 the Ithaca Railway Company laid tracks uphill as far as Stewart Avenue. By September the Company was permitted by Cornell to continue its route from the end of Eddy Street along a private right-of-way behind Cascadilla Hall to College Avenue before crossing a private bridge to the campus. An additional span continued the line from the northern end of College Avenue to the east end of Oak Avenue, and on to the Elmira, Cortland and Northern railroad depot on Maple Avenue.

In 1903, to satisfy a burgeoning need for student housing, Charles L. Sheldon, class of 1901, purchased the large lot southeast of Cascadilla Hall and constructed a private men's dormitory. Designed by Henry W. Wilkinson, class of 1890, the building housed 135 students in single rooms and suites. Sheldon Court also contained the Triangle Book Shop, a physician's office, and a restaurant known as Mother's Kitchen.

Sheldon Court, 412-420 College Avenue

SHELDON COURT eventually passed into the hands of Sheldon's son and daughter. Mary Sheldon Lyon became a follower of Father Divine, a charismatic Black religious leader, and took the name Dove Peace. Upon her death at the age of 85 her half interest in the property passed to the religious group. In 1948 Evan J. Morris, owner of the Triangle Book Shop, purchased the building from the Angels of Father Divine. Seven years later Cornell acquired the building. With the addition of another story in 1981, the building returned to its original use as a college dormitory with shops on the ground floor.

Cascadilla Hall (c.1898)

IN 1864 Ezra Cornell proposed the establishment of a water cure or sanitarium at Cascadilla Creek, hoping to promote Ithaca as a health resort. In cooperation with Dr. Samantha Nivison, a proprietor of a water cure at Dryden Springs, Cornell supervised and substantially financed the construction of a building known as The Cascadilla, near the site of Otis Eddy's cotton mill. Designed by Albany architects Nichols and Brown, the building was constructed in 1866 of stone quarried from the adjacent gorge below the Central Avenue Bridge. However the idea of a water cure was soon abandoned. In 1869 partial ownership of the building was transferred to the University and it was used for student and faculty housing. Cascadilla enjoyed a high rate of occupancy, though boarders paid between five and seven dollars a week for room and board in the 1870's, considerably higher than the rates charged by neighboring boarding houses on College Avenue. In 1884 the top floor was remodelled with an oriel window and new entrance at the south side of the building were added according to plans by William Henry Miller.

Cascadilla Hall

IN 1963 Cascadilla Hall was remodelled for use as a graduate student dormitory. In 1982 the structure underwent a $7,200,000 alteration: the interior was gutted and renovated, the original roof was removed, and two new floors were added. The building now houses undergraduate students.

Arts Quad, Cornell University, Looking North from McGraw Tower (1902)

THE DESIGN of the Cornell campus was the result of the careful and prodigious planning of three men: Ezra Cornell, the founder of the University; Andrew D. White, Cornell's first president; and Frederick Law Olmsted, the prominent landscape architect and the University's first landscape adviser. White envisioned a campus designed in large quadrangles, and the early development of the University followed that form. The Arts Quadrangle, photographed from high atop the roof of McGraw Tower in this image, is bounded on the west by the University's first three buildings, Morrill Hall, McGraw Hall and White Hall, erected in 1866, 1867 and 1869 respectively. All three buildings were designed to front a terrace facing the west that was never built. West Sibley Hall, located at the northern end of the Quad, was erected in 1870 to house the College of Mechanical Engineering. In 1884 West Sibley Hall was nearly doubled in size. Ten years later East Sibley Hall was built for the rapidly expanding college. At the time this photograph was taken, Sibley Dome, linking East and West Sibley Halls, was under construction. Designed by Arthur Gibb, the dome contained a large auditorium and a museum. To the west of Sibley stands Franklin Hall, built in 1882 for the physics and chemistry departments. Additional space required by the chemistry department led to the erection of Morse Hall, adjacent to Franklin, in 1888. Lincoln Hall, at the eastern edge of the Quad, was built in the same year to house the Schools of Civil Engineering and Architecture.

Arts Quad, Cornell University, Looking North from McGraw Tower

THIS QUADRANGLE has not been significantly altered since A. D. White's original conception. The only brick building on the Quad, Morse Hall was partially destroyed by fire in February 1916. It was demolished in 1954. In 1970 construction began on the Johnson Museum of Art, designed by architect I. M. Pei. After some debate, the museum, shown at the left edge of the photograph, was sited on the promontory where in 1866 Ezra Cornell first persuaded the Trustees to build the University.

Stone Hall, Roberts Hall, and East Roberts Hall, Cornell University (c.1907)

THE FIRST courses in agriculture at Cornell University, mandated by the Morrill Land Grant Act of 1862, were held in Morrill Hall on the Arts Quad. A bachelor's degree in Agriculture was first offered in 1872. Isaac P. Roberts was an appointed Professor of Agriculture in the 1870's and became Director of the College of Agriculture upon its creation in 1888. In 1891, 22 undergraduate students were enrolled in the agricultural program at the University. With the appointment of Liberty Hyde Bailey as the Dean of the College of Agriculture in 1903, the program became a major component of the University. In 1904, $250,000 was appropriated by New York State for the erection of buildings for the College. George H. Heins, appointed the first State Architect by Governor Theodore Roosevelt in 1898, designed the new buildings. The State Legislature specified the construction of a main building, not to cost more than $125,000, and buildings for agricultural machinery, stock-judging, and horticulture. Construction of Stone Hall, Roberts Hall, and East Roberts Hall began in 1905 on a site east of Garden Avenue. Dedication of the buildings took place in April of 1907. Stone Hall housed the Department of Rural Education. Roberts Hall, the principal building, contained the administrative offices for the College of Agriculture, classrooms, and the Horticulture, Entomology, and Home Economic Departments. East Roberts was the dairy building.

East Side of Garden Avenue at Tower Road

ENROLLMENT in the College of Agriculture increased dramatically during the first decade of the twentieth century, requiring additional buildings. Six new structures were erected with state funds in the years 1912 and 1913: Comstock Hall for home economics; Rice Hall for poultry husbandry; Wing Hall for animal husbandry; Caldwell Hall for soils science; Fernow Hall for forestry; and Bailey Hall. The buildings were sited according to the campus master plan prepared by Manning and Fleming in 1910. In the academic year 1912-1913 the College of Agriculture was the largest college in the University. The foreground shadows in the photograph are cast by the building of the School of Industrial and Labor Relations. Shown on the right is the Seeley G. Mudd Hall, constructed in 1982. Today the oldest buildings on the Ag Quad, East Roberts, Roberts, and Stone are threatened with demolition as the University pursues plans for new construction adjacent to the site.

South Side of State Street at Base of East Hill (1934)

THE FIRST automobile in Ithaca was driven down Seneca Street by Raymond Bettys of Rochester in June 1899 to the shock and bewilderment of many observers. There were only 954 automobiles in all of New York State in 1903, the first year vehicular registration began. By 1920 enough people owned automobiles in Ithaca to support fifteen garages. Throughout the 1920's many of Ithaca's older homes, located on major thoroughfares, were replaced by service stations. As shown in this photo, East State Street, north of Aurora Street, once lined with stately early nineteenth century residences, was soon dotted with gasoline stations, eager to service car owners before they headed up the hill. In the year this photograph was taken, 11,348 passenger vehicles were registered in Tompkins County, and Ithaca had 39 gasoline stations. The large five-story cast concrete structure in the distance was erected in 1924 by Harry Dean, President of Dean of Ithaca, a storage warehouse firm.

South Side of State Street at Base of East Hill

By THE 1950's, the remaining residences on this block had been demolished and their sites left vacant. The extension in 1956 of Green and Seneca Streets to the base of the State Street hill markedly changed downtown traffic patterns. This stretch of State Street, between South Aurora Street and the Dean of Ithaca building, was cleared by 1972. Travelers up the hill now stop for a pizza instead of gasoline. The existing brick paving, installed in 1941, is one of only two brick streets remaining in Ithaca. The City Board of Public Works has recommended repaving the street with asphalt.

(1905)

(1907)

(1983)

Six Mile Creek and South Hill, Looking Southwest from State Street

WHEN THE Ithaca Street Railway Company began its operations in 1887, its car barns were located across from the Lehigh Valley railroad station at the west end of the line. In 1893 the former Brush-Swan Electric Light Company power house, located at the foot of State Street on Six Mile Creek, was renovated for use as a trolley car barn and substation. Although a flood in December 1901 caused the south wall of the car barn to be swept into the creek, the structure was rebuilt. On June 21, 1905, a ten hour torrential rainstorm caused serious flooding along Six Mile Creek, especially that area between the car barns and Cayuga Street. The car barns were heavily damaged, and portions of the retaining wall erected after the 1901 flood were washed away. Most of the lumber washed up along the bank came from sheds along the creek. In the winter of 1907 the retaining wall behind the car barns were rebuilt, as is pictured in the photograph. Wood stacked in the foreground was used to construct forms for poured concrete retaining walls.

THE ITHACA Railway Company began bus operation in May of 1935. The last trolley ran on June 22, 1935, bringing to an end 48 years of trolley service in Ithaca. The car barn was then used as a garage for the buses until the late 1950's. Eventually the site was purchased by Wilcox Press and the barn was used as a warehouse. Flooding in the summer of 1981 again undermined the retaining walls of this section of Six Mile Creek, which have been rebuilt. In January of 1982 the remaining western brick portion of the building was demolished. The photograph shows the roof of Wilcox Press including special pollution abatement equipment recently installed.

ITHACA'S GROWTH by the mid-nineteenth century necessitated an organized water system for a community that had previously relied upon individual private wells. The Ithaca Light and Water Company was established in 1853 and water was fed from Cascadilla Creek to "springs" on East Hill, where it was pumped down East Buffalo Street through small iron lines. The company was purchased by the Treman family in the early 1860's. By the early 1870's water was supplied to the city from Buttermilk Creek. Use of Six Mile Creek for city water supply began in 1872 when the company purchased a dam at Van Nattas mill at Giles Street. A pumping station built there the following year supplied water to East Hill. In order to provide purer water, higher pressure to hillside homes, and better fire protection, construction of a dam just outside the city on Six Mile Creek began on September 11, 1902. An impounding reservoir capable of holding 72,000,000 gallons was created by a 30-foot reinforced concrete dam. This photograph shows the dam before the reservoir filled. A 24-inch pipeline leading from the bottom of the reservoir carried water to the purification plant a mile away on Water Street southwest of State Street. The new system began operation on August 19, 1903, and three days later the supply from Buttermilk Creek was shut off.

30-Foot Dam,
Six Mile Creek (1903)

IT WAS WIDELY believed that the unsanitary conditions prevalent during the construction of the 30-Foot Dam contributed to the typhoid epidemic which hit the city in January of 1903, resulting in 85 deaths. As a result of public outcry, the City of Ithaca acquired ownership of the private water works system from the Treman family in 1904 at a cost of $900,000. Steps were immediately taken to upgrade the network. New high-powered pumping machinery and a new dam were installed at Van Nattas in 1906. In 1911 the Potters Falls upper reservoir was built, located one and one-half miles east of the city and capable of holding 350,000,000 gallons of water. As pictured in this photograph, the control house at the lower reservoir feeding the pipeline down Six Mile Creek has been rebuilt with concrete block, and the brickwork along the gorge has deteriorated.

30-Foot Dam,
Six Mile Creek

Catskill Turnpike, Looking East at City Limits (1898)

In 1804 the Catskill Turnpike, extending from Catskill on the Hudson River to Bath in Steuben County, became a state public highway, signed into law by Governor George Clinton. The turnpike passed through Ithaca on Owego (now State) Street, and provided the primary means of access to this area before the establishment of railroads. Tolls on the turnpike were collected every ten miles, but numerous exemptions were allowed such as, "no charge for a person passing to or from public worship, his farm, or a funeral, or to or from a grist-mill for grinding grain for the family's use, or to or from a blacksmith's shop to which he usually resorts, or any person residing within four miles of said gate, or going for or returning with a physician, or attending election."[12] Toll collectors charged 8 cents for every score of sheep or hogs, 20 cents for every score of cattle, horses, or mules, 6 cents for carts drawn by one horse, 25 cents for each chariot, coach or phaeton, and 12½ cents for every cart drawn by two oxen. In this view the photographer's horse and buggy wait to the side of the muddy Catskill Turnpike (now Slaterville Road) at the eastern boundary of the city.

New York State Route 79, Looking East at City Limits

TODAY TRAFFIC along the route of the Catskill Turnpike is considerably faster and more frequent, and the photographer can no longer stand in the middle of the road to record the identical view. The original turnpike route can still be followed, though changes have been made to the road to eliminate hazardous curves and grades. The two residences and a barn visible in the historic view remain, though the far buildings are obscured by trees, and new neighboring structures on small lots line New York State Route 79.

FOOTNOTES

1. J. A. Miller, ed., *Ithaca, N. Y. as a City of Residence and Manufacture* (Ithaca: J. A. Miller and Company, 1891), p. 32.

2. Quoted in Arthur E. Niedeck, "A Sketch of the Theatres of Ithaca 1842-1942," presented to the DeWitt Historical Society of Tompkins County, Inc., 23 March 1943, p. 3.

3. *Ithaca Daily Journal*, 10 July 1896, p. 6.

4. Quoted in *Ithaca Daily News*, 15 February 1919, p. 7.

5. J. A. Miller, ed., *Ithaca, N. Y. as a City of Residence and Manufacture* (Ithaca: J. A. Miller and Company, 1891), p. 43.

6. *The Ithaca Directory for 1875-6* (Ithaca: O. H. Bame and Company, 1875), p. 12.

7. Arthur E. Niedeck, "A Sketch of the Theatres of Ithaca 1842-1942," presented to the DeWitt Historical Society of Tompkins County, Inc., 23 March 1943, p. 72.

8. "Ithaca YMCA History," *Ithaca Journal* 23-29 November 1968, Ithaca YMCA 100th Birthday Special Section, p. 9.

9. John H. Selkreg, ed., *Landmarks of Tompkins County* (Syracuse: D. Mason and Company, 1894), part II, p. 38.

10. Quoted in Thomas W. Burns, *Initial Ithacans* (Ithaca: Press of the Ithaca Journal, 1904), p. 139.

11. *Ithaca Journal*, 22 June 1935, p. 3.

12. *Ithaca Journal News*, 24 January 1925, p. 8.

BIBLIOGRAPHY

Abt, Henry Edward. *Ithaca, Its Origin and Growth*. Ithaca: Ross W. Kellogg, 1926.

Annual Report of the Board of Education of the City of Ithaca. Ithaca: Board of Education, 1909, 1913, 1914.

Annual Report of the Board of Education of the Village of Ithaca. Ithaca: Andrus and Church, 1885, 1887.

Bishop, Morris. *A History of Cornell*. Ithaca: Cornell University Press, 1962.

Burns, Thomas W. *Initial Ithacans*. Ithaca: Press of the Ithaca Journal, 1904.

Clarke, F. W. *Views Around Ithaca*. Ithaca: Andrus, McChain and Company, 1869.

Goodwin, Hermon Camp. *Ithaca As It Was, and Ithaca As It Is*. Ithaca: Andrus, Gauntlett and Company, 1853.

Harris, Dorothy. *History of Ithaca's Water and Sewer Systems*. Ithaca: Department of Public Works, 1956.

Ithaca Chronological Historical Events. Springfield, Mass.: H. A. Manning Company, 1939.

Ithaca City Directories, 1864-present.

Jaeger, A. Robert. "Historic Structure Report, The Sprague House, Ithaca, New York," Ithaca, 1982.

Jehn, Dorothy. "The Clinton House, Ithaca, New York, An Historical and Rehabilitation Analysis." M.A. Thesis, Cornell University, 1964.

Kerr, Richard D. *The Ithaca Street Railway*. Forty Fort, Pa.: Harold E. Cox, 1972.

Kurtz, D. Morris. *Ithaca and Its Resources*. Ithaca: Journal Association Book and Job Print, 1883.

Lee, Hardy Campbell and Winton Rossiter. *A History of Railroads in Tompkins County*. Ithaca: DeWitt Historical Society of Tompkins County, 1977.

Miller, J. A., ed. *Ithaca, N. Y. as a City of Residence and Manufacture*. Ithaca: J. A. Miller, 1891.

The National Bank of Newburgh 1811-1911. New York: H. K. Brewer and Company, 1911.

Niedeck, Arthur E. "A Sketch of the Theatres of Ithaca 1842-1942." Presented to the DeWitt Historical Society of Tompkins County, Inc., 23 March 1943.

Norris, W. Glenn. *The Origin of Place Names in Tompkins County*. Ithaca: DeWitt Historical Society of Tompkins County, 1951.

Parsons, Kermit Carlyle. *The Cornell Campus*. Ithaca: Cornell University Press, 1962.

Peirce, Henry D. and Hamilton Hurd. *History of Tioga, Chemung, Tompkins, and Schuyler Counties, New York*. Philadelphia: Everts and Ensign, 1879.

Rash, David. "Chronological Listing of Architectural Articles and Notations in the *Ithaca Daily Journal*, January 1890-December 1909." Ithaca, 1981.

Sachse, Gretchen, Janet Mara and Gretel Leed. *The Spirit of Enterprise: Nineteenth Century in Tompkins County*. Ithaca: Hinckley Foundation Museum, 1977.

Selkreg, John H. *Landmarks of Tompkins County, New York*. Syracuse: D. Mason and Company, 1894.

Sixth Annual Report of the Commissioners of the Ithaca Fire Department. Ithaca: Press of the Ithaca Daily News, 1900.

Snodderly, Daniel R. *Ithaca and Its Past*. Ithaca: DeWitt Historical Society of Tompkins County, 1982.

Southwick, Solomon. *Views of Ithaca and Its Environs*. Ithaca: D. D. and A. Spencer, 1835.

Spencer, Spence, ed. *The Scenery of Ithaca*. Ithaca: Spence Spencer, 1866.

Stephenson, Jean and Ellsworth Filby. *The Land of the Finger Lakes.* Ithaca: Cornell University Press, 1917.

Thurber, Charles Herbert. *In and Out of Ithaca.* Ithaca: Andrus and Church, 1887.

Whitford, Noble E. *History of the Barge Canal of New York State.* Albany: J. B. Lyon Company, 1922.

Whitford, Noble E. *History of the Canal System of the State of New York.* Albany: Brandow Printing Company, 1906.

Wright, Russell. "A Feasibility Study of the Potential Rehabilitation of Roberts, East Roberts and Stone Halls, New York State College of Agriculture and Life Sciences, Cornell University, Ithaca, New York." Prepared for Historic Ithaca, Inc., 1981.

HISTORIC PHOTO CREDITS

Joseph C. Burritt, frontispiece, p. 38

Robert G. Estabrook, p. 30

Henry Head, pp. 74, 82, 86

Charles H. Howes, p. 46

Ellsworth McGillvray, pp. 48, 80, 92

Seth L. Sheldon, pp. 14, 18, 32, 34, 64, 70; attributed to Sheldon, pp. 10, 12, 16, 22 top, 22 bottom, 24, 26, 28, 36, 42, 44, 50 top, 50 bottom, 56, 60, 62, 66, 68, 88 top, 88 bottom, 90

Warrington R. Tompkins, p. 20

Unattributed, pp. 8, 40 top, 40 bottom, 52, 54, 58, 72, 76, 78, 84

BIOGRAPHICAL NOTES

MERRILL HESCH, an Art History graduate of Vassar College, has been active in research and photographic documentation of historic buildings in New York State for the past six years. Between 1977 and 1979 she worked on the Schermerhorn Row Block restoration project in lower Manhattan. Merrill moved to Ithaca in 1979 to pursue graduate study in City and Regional Planning at Cornell University. She is currently a Field Representative for the New York State Division for Historic Preservation in New York City.

RICHARD PIEPER graduated from Cornell University with a degree in Geochemistry in 1971. He worked as a restoration carpenter in Tompkins County before moving to New York City, where he participated in the extensive documentation effort of the Schermerhorn Row Block. In 1981 Pieper studied architectural conservation at the International Center for the Study of the Preservation and Restoration of Cultural Property in Rome, Italy. Pieper is currently employed as Architectural Conservator for Historic Ithaca and Tompkins County, a non-profit preservation organization, and the Department of Planning and Development, City of Ithaca.